**BUG BOOKS**

# Snail

### Karen Hartley
### and
### Chris Macro

D1335843

**Heinemann**
LIBRARY

First published in Great Britain by Heinemann Library
Halley Court, Jordan Hill, Oxford OX2 8EJ
a division of Reed Educational and Professional Publishing Ltd.
Heinemann is a registered trademark of Reed Educational & Professional Publishing Limited.

OXFORD FLORENCE PRAGUE MADRID ATHENS
MELBOURNE AUCKLAND KUALA LUMPUR SINGAPORE TOKYO
IBADAN NAIROBI KAMPALA JOHANNESBURG GABORONE
PORTSMOUTH NH CHICAGO MEXICO CITY SAO PAULO

Designed by Celia Floyd
Illustrations by Alan Male
Printed in Hong Kong / China

02 01 00 99
10 9 8 7 6 5 4 3 2

ISBN 0 431 01681 X
This title is also available in a hardback library edition (ISBN 0 431 01674 7)

**British Library Cataloguing in Publication Data**

Hartley, Karen
    Snail. - (Bug books)
    1.Snails - Juvenile literature
    I. Title II. Macro, Chris
    593.3

**Acknowledgements**
The Publishers would like to thank the following for permission to reproduce photographs: Ardea London Ltd: pp14, 26, J Daniels p8, J Mason p13, P Morris p4; Bruce Coleman Ltd: J Burton pp24, 25, W Layer p23, H Reinhard p15, K Taylor pp11, 16, 18; FLPA: A Wharton p20; Chris Honeywell pp28, 29; Nature Photographers Ltd: P Sterry p12; NHPA: M Tweedie p10; Oxford Scientific Films: G Bernard p27; M Birkhead p9, L Crowhurst p7, W Gray p19, J Pontier p5, T Tilford p22; Planet Earth Pictures: S Hopkins pp6, 21; Premaphotos: K Preston-Mafham p17

Cover photograph reproduced with permission of child: Chris Honeywell; snail: M Mattock/Telegraph Colour Library

Every effort has been made to contact copyright holders of any material reproduced in this book. Any omissions will be rectified in subsequent printings if notice is given to the Publisher.

Any words appearing in the text in bold, **like this**, are explained in the Glossary.

# Contents

# What are snails?

Snails have a soft body and carry a hard shell. They do not have any legs. Some snails live in water but in this book we will be looking at snails that live in gardens and woods.

Snails come in different sizes and have shells of different colours. Some snails are very small. Some are very big. This is a Giant African land snail. It can grow to be longer than your foot!

# What do snails look like?

Snails have a thick, soft **foot** that they can pull into their hard shell. Each ring on the shell is called a **whorl**. The soft foot usually feels damp and slimy.

Snails have a mouth under their head and a breathing hole under their shell. The short **feelers** are for touch and smell. The long ones have two tiny eyes at the end.

# How big are snails?

Adult garden snails are nearly as long as one of your middle fingers when they are moving. Baby snails are about the size of your little fingernail.

Snails are much smaller when they are inside their shells. As snails grow, their shells get bigger.

# How are snails born?

Snails make a hole in the soil and lay eggs there. They usually lay about 40 eggs at a time. The eggs are white.

After about 21 days, the eggs **hatch** and the baby snails begin to move about. They have little shells and very **pale** bodies.

# How do snails grow?

The snail's body gets darker as it gets older. In the first year the shell has about three **whorls**. Can you see them?

The snail is fully grown when it is about 2 years old. It will have about five whorls on its shell.

# What do snails eat?

Snails like to eat leaves or plants which are brown and smelly. If there are no dead leaves then snails will eat fresh, green plants.

Sometimes snails eat the green **algae** off the branches of trees. Some snails will even eat other snails but they prefer to eat plants.

# Which animals attack snails?

Snails' enemies usually attack at night. Rats, large beetles and ducks like to eat snails. Some birds break open the snail's shell on stones and then peck at the soft body.

When a snail thinks it is in danger it will hide in its shell. Sometimes it makes **froth** come out from under the shell to scare off its attackers.

# Where do snails live?

Many snails live in gardens. They also live in woods, hedges and in grass. They like damp, dark places.

You can often find snails under stones. After it has been raining you may see them climbing up walls. Snails can cling very tightly to walls and stones.

# How do snails move?

Snails move slowly. They move quicker when it is warm and wet. The muscles in the **foot** make the snail move. Can you see the muscles in this foot?

Snails make slime to help them to slide over rough paths and stones. They make more slime when they are on slopes or rough ground.

# How long do snails live?

If snails live where there are lots of enemies then they do not live for very long. Can you see the empty shells? The snails have been eaten.

Some garden snails can live for 5 years. Some **desert** snails can stay in their shells for years, without eating or moving. They live much longer than busy garden snails.

# What do snails do?

Snails come out when the weather is damp. When the weather is very hot snails stop eating and bury themselves. Snails will also hide if the weather is very cold.

Snails like to look for food at night.
They feel safer in the dark.

# How are snails special?

Snails can smell strong smells through their **feelers**. If a snail smells something it does not like, it goes into its shell. Sometimes snails like to stay very close together.

When snails go to sleep for the winter, or when it is hot, they make a skin over the opening of the shell. This is called the **epiphragm**.

# Thinking about snails

Which food do you think the snail will like best? What are the snails' **feelers** used for?

Which surface do you think the snail likes best? Will the snail make more slime when it is moving on the carpet or on the smooth wood?

How do you think the snail moves?

# Bug map

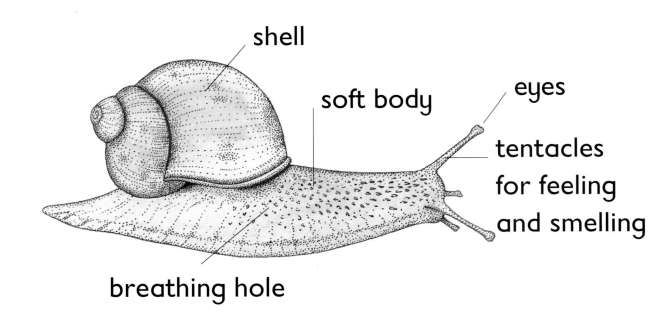

shell

soft body

eyes

tentacles for feeling and smelling

breathing hole

# Glossary

**algae** a green slime which grows on the branches and trunks of trees

**desert** bare land that has little or no rainfall

**epiphragm** the skin which the snail makes to cover the opening of its shell

**feelers** long thin tubes on a snail's head. These are used for feeling and smelling. The eyes are at the end of one pair of feelers.

**foot** the soft body of the snail that comes out of the shell

**froth** a white foam which snails make when in danger. This comes out from under the shell.

**hatch** to come out of the egg

**pale** light in colour, almost white

**whorls** the rings on a snail's shell

# Index